Daily Life

Pirates

Other books in the Daily Life series are:

The American Colonies
Ancient Rome
The Gold Rush
The Oregon Trail
A Plains Indian Village

Daily Life

Pirates

Patricia D. Netzley

KidHaven Press

KidHaven Press, an imprint of Gale Group, Inc.
10911 Technology Place, San Diego, CA 92127

Picture Credits

Cover Photo: © Herbert Morton Stoops/Wood River Galley/PictureQuest
© Paul Almasy/CORBIS, 21
© Archivo Iconographico, S.A./CORBIS, 22
Associated Press, 28
© Bettman/CORBIS, 39 (bottom)
Mary Evans Picture Library, 10, 16, 18, 30, 32, 37, 39 (top), 41
Chris Jouan, 13, 35
© Charles & Josette Lenars/CORBIS, 7
© The Newberry Library/Stock Montage, Inc., 11
© North Wind Picture Archives, 8, 9, 20, 34
Private Collection/ Bridgeman Art Library, 26
Private Collection/ Christie's Images/Bridgeman Art Library, 29
Royal Geographical Society, London, UK/Bridgeman Art Library, 25

Library of Congress Cataloging-in-Publication Data

Netzley, Patricia D.
  Pirates / by Patricia D. Netzley.
    p. cm. — (Daily life)
  Includes bibliographical references and index.
  Summary: Discusses the daily life of pirates including life
onboard ship, attacking and robbing other ships, and time
spent onshore.
    ISBN 0-7377-0937-5 (hardback)
    1. Pirates—Juvenile literature. [1. Pirates.] I. Title. II. Series.
  G535 .N47 2002
  910 . 4'5—dc21

                                                              2001003816

Contents

Chapter One

The Ship and Its Crew

For as long as merchants have been sending money and goods by ship, seagoing thieves called pirates have robbed them. The ancient Greeks, Romans, and Egyptians had trouble with pirates in the Mediterranean Sea, and in medieval times the English, French, Portuguese, Spanish, Chinese, and Japanese all had to fight piracy along their shores. Pirate attacks increased steadily during the sixteenth, seventeenth, and eighteenth centuries, not only near coastlines but also throughout the Atlantic and Indian Oceans.

Becoming a Pirate

In fact, pirates were so successful in the seventeenth and eighteenth centuries that this period is now known as the golden age of piracy. Some of the golden-age pirates were hired by one country to attack the ships of other countries. These hired pirates were called **privateers**, and in their own countries they were often respected gentlemen.

Most pirates, however, worked only for themselves. Pirates of all different nationalities often sailed together

Piracy dates back as far as the days of ancient Greece.

on one ship. Some were runaway slaves, while others were escaped convicts. Most, however, were seamen who had deserted merchant or naval ships, which had low pay and poor working conditions. Sometimes the entire crew of such a ship would turn to piracy after getting rid of a cruel captain. Between 1715 and 1737 this happened at least twenty times.

Pirates who captured a ship rarely forced its ordinary sailors to join their crew, although many chose to do so. Pirates did, however, often force people with special skills such as carpentry to remain onboard. Musicians were especially prized because they could entertain the men at sea. Old men, though, were rarely encouraged to join a pirate crew because sailing a ship required physical strength and agility. The average age of a pirate was twenty-seven.

Pirate Clothes

To make it easier to work on board ship, most pirates wore loose clothing. The most common outfit was a wool jacket, a linen or sailcloth shirt, and baggy ankle- or knee-length wool, cotton, or sailcloth pants. Some pirate pants were so baggy they looked like skirts. Such clothing made it possible for women to work as pirates. Since most ships did not allow women on board (even wives), female pirates had to disguise themselves as men, and the looser their clothing, the easier it was for them to do this.

Meanwhile, pirate captains typically wore colorful clothes in expensive fabrics like silk or velvet. For example, Bartholomew Roberts sailed the Atlantic in a red velvet coat, a hat with a red feather, and lots of gold and diamond jewelry. Some pirates wore such clothing when going ashore but not onboard ship because it was not practical.

Before fighting a battle, many pirate captains tried to make themselves look frightening. One captain known as Blackbeard, for instance, would stick slow-burning cords under his hat and set them on fire so that smoke would

Female pirates disguised themselves as men.

Blackbeard burned cords under his hat to create a frightening appearance.

billow around his head to scare his victims. Captain Philip Lyne only had to look at his victims to scare them. According to an article in the *Boston Gazette* newspaper of March 28, 1726, Lyne had "one eye shot out, which with part of his nose, hung down on his face."[1]

The Ship's Crew

However, even the most fearsome captain was subject to the wishes of his crew. A pirate ship belonged to everyone on board, and the crew elected the captain by popular vote. Once elected, the captain's job was only to lead sea battles. As pirate Walter Kennedy said of his shipmates in 1721: "They chose a captain from amongst themselves, who in effect held little more than that title, excepting in an engagement [of battle], when he commanded absolutely and without control [of his passions]."[2]

Sometimes pirates fought one another to determine who would be captain of a ship.

Bartholomew Roberts preferred piracy to an honest living.

A captain who made too many mistakes would soon be voted out of office. One ship replaced its captain thirteen times in less than six months. Although pirate captains took the blame when anything went wrong, most did not regret being chosen for the job. Pirate captain Bartholomew Roberts, for example, once said, "It is better to be a commander than a common man, since I have dipped my hands in muddy water and must be a pirate."[3]

A pirate crew also elected its captain's assistant, known as the **quartermaster.** The quartermaster was in charge of rationing supplies, and he led groups going ashore to look for food and water. He also commanded boarding parties onto ships that had just been attacked, and then he decided which goods to take and how to divide them into equal shares. When the pirate crew voted to keep a captured ship, the quartermaster was usually given the job of captaining it at least until it was sold.

The quartermaster also settled disputes and punished pirates who broke the ship's rules. The typical punishment was a **flogging**, or whipping, with a cat-o'-nine-tails, a rope with nine strands. Usually the end of each strand was tied in a knot, but sometimes the knot held a fishhook or a ball of metal to make the whipping more painful. Only the quartermaster was allowed to flog someone, and he could not do this until everybody on the ship had voted on whether the wrongdoer deserved a flogging and on how many times he should be struck.

Other jobs on a pirate ship included cook, sailing master (who was both the navigator and the person in charge of setting the sails), carpenter, and surgeon. Two of the most important jobs were **gunner** and **bosun**. The gunner maintained the ship's weapons and managed its ammunition. The bosun, also called a boatswain, inspected the rigging every day and issued orders related to the use and repair of all ropes.

Pirate Ships

Pirates sailed on whatever ships they could steal that were worth keeping. However, they preferred fast ships because there was no way to rob someone you could not catch. Therefore, most chose to sail a **sloop**, a one-masted ship that could go about 12.5 miles per hour (or, in sailing terms, about 11 knots) in a good wind. Between 1710 and 1730, more than half of all pirate attacks in the western Atlantic Ocean were committed by sloops. There were many types of sloops, but historians do not know exactly which types were favored by pirates.

The next most popular pirate vessel was the **ship**. Today the word *ship* refers to many kinds of seagoing vessels, but in the seventeenth and eighteenth centuries it referred only to a vessel with square sails on three or more masts. Although ships were not as fast as sloops, they could have crews of at least two hundred whereas sloops usually held no more than seventy-five. Meanwhile, most merchant ships had crews of less than twenty men, so pirates on either sloops or ships easily outnumbered their victims.

Pirates also preferred to have crews of 100 to 250 men because they usually added dozens of extra guns to their vessels, and each gun required 4 to 6 men to position, load, aim, and fire it. Pirates made many

Sailing Ships

Full-Rigged Ship

Sloop

other changes to ships as well, such as removing any buildings on deck. Without buildings, they had more room to fight invaders, who had no place to hide.

Pirates used whatever tactics were necessary to increase their chances of success. However, few became rich from their efforts. A pirate's life was very hard, and many wasted their money on alcohol and gambling while trying to forget their troubles. Others died on the open seas or were caught and executed by governments tired of their piracy. Still, many pirates continued to hope that the next ship they attacked would bring them the great wealth and happiness they so desired.

Chapter Two

The Rigors of Life at Sea

Many pirates had previous sailing experience on-board merchant or naval vessels. For them, life on a pirate ship was an improvement because more hands were onboard to share the work and everyone had a vote in what took place. However, there were still many difficulties to endure and rules to follow.

Pirate Rules

During the golden age, every pirate ship had rules, although they differed slightly from ship to ship. These rules told how stolen goods should be divided and how pirates should behave on board ship. For example, the rules on Bartholomew Roberts's ship included that "the lights and candles to be put out at eight o'clock at night: if any of the crew, after that hour still remained inclined for drinking, they were to do it on the open deck."[4]

Roberts's rules also stated that someone caught running away during battle would be punished with death or marooning, which involved stranding the wrongdoer on a deserted island or in a tiny boat with few supplies. On the pirate ship *Revenge*, marooning was the punishment for any pirate caught stealing from another, and any pirate caught striking another was flogged.

Some pirate ships had a rule that drinking was only allowed on deck.

Difficult Living Conditions

Despite rules against hitting, pirates often got into fist-fights. One reason for this was the men's crowded living conditions. As many as 250 pirates might sleep side by side on a ship only 127 feet long and 40 feet wide. They had no privacy, even while using the toilet. Sometimes these facilities were buckets, but other times they were wooden boxes with holes overhanging the water so that waste would drop into the sea.

Animal waste was a more serious problem. Most ships had live goats, ducks, geese, and chickens in their hold so that the men could have fresh meat to eat, and in good weather the goats were allowed to roam the deck. In addition, many pirates kept pets like dogs and parrots.

Cleaning up after all of these animals was difficult. To wash floors and decks, pirates used a mixture of vinegar and seawater or sometimes brandy or other alcoholic drinks. Still, some parts of the ship never got completely clean. Waste and spilled food collected between floorboards and in places so dark that sailors could not see them. This attracted rats, cockroaches, and beetles, which, along with fleas, made the pirates' lives miserable. To get rid of these pests belowdecks, pirates would fill pans with material that burned easily and set it on fire, hoping the smoke would drive the creatures away. Even when this worked, the rats and insects soon returned.

Another problem belowdecks was dampness. Every wooden ship leaked a little, and during heavy storms

Pirate ships were crowded and provided no privacy.

even more seawater would slosh inside from up on deck. Since no sunlight could reach the hold, it never dried out. Anyone who slept there often found himself with wet blankets and clothes.

Illnesses and Bad Food

Under such conditions, many pirates caught colds. They also caught more serious diseases, such as typhoid, malaria, and yellow fever, which spread rapidly on board crowded, unclean ships. On long voyages a pirate ship could easily lose half its crew to sickness. In addition, many pirates developed **scurvy**, an illness caused by not getting enough vitamin C. To prevent this illness, pirate ships typically carried limes, which are rich in vitamin C.

Pirates who were sick were usually given food treats such as almonds, jellies, and currants. Otherwise, they ate poorly on long voyages, since there was no easy way to preserve the meat from animals killed on board. These animals included not only livestock but also fish, sea tortoises, dolphins, and porpoises harpooned at sea. For times when fresh meat was not available, pirates stocked their ship with dried, salted meat, which remained edible for a long time. Pirate ships also carried **hardtack**, a dry, hard biscuit that would last for months if stored properly.

Getting Fresh Water

Another item that quickly went bad was fresh water, which was kept in wooden barrels. Once the water became stale, the barrel had to be emptied, cleaned, and refilled. This meant that the pirates had to take the empty barrel to shore in a rowboat, find a stream, fill the barrel up with water, and then row it back to the ship. Sometimes problems arose during this ordeal. For instance, John Esquemeling, who sailed on a pirate ship during the early seventeenth century, wrote,

> I went with ten more of our company and two canoes, to fetch water from the land. Having filled our jars, we could not get back to the ship by reason of . . . [bad weather]. . . . [That night] we ventured out both canoes together but the winds were

Alcohol was a common substitute for fresh water.

so high that we were forced to throw all our jars of water overboard to lighten our boats—otherwise we would have inevitably perished.[5]

Drinking and Gambling

Faced with such difficulties, many pirates chose to supplement their water supply with barrels of beer, wine, or rum because alcohol does not spoil. However, these beverages made the crew drunk, which created more problems. On Roberts's ship, for example, many crewmen were never sober enough to climb up into the rigging to tend the sails.

Besides drinking, some pirates spent a lot of time betting money on card and dice games. Sometimes they

To pass the time, pirates played card games with cards like these.

were so busy gambling that they neglected their work, losing small fortunes in the process. On Esquemeling's ship, gambling crewmen lost about 260,000 Spanish coins called "**pieces of eight**" within a period of three weeks. Just ten of these coins were enough to buy a small herd of cows. Gambling also caused many fights to break out, even between friends. For these reasons, many vessels forbade crewmen from placing bets on board ship.

Rough Seas

Playing cards helped to pass the time when the winds were calm. Otherwise, there was much work to do.

Storms at sea and shipwrecks killed many pirates.

Getting a large wooden sailing ship from one place to another involved many steps. In fact, one sailor who tried to write them all down came up with over one hundred pages of instructions.

All of these steps were more difficult in rough weather, and storms at sea were common. This was especially true in the western Atlantic Ocean, where many shipwrecks occurred. The most famous pirate wreck in this area was that of the *Whydah* off the coast of New England in 1717. Captained by Sam Bellamy, the *Whydah* got caught in a storm with gale-force winds, hit a shoal, and broke apart. Captain Bellamy and all but 2 of his 143 men died in the wreck. Another pirate crew survived a similar storm by throwing all guns and goods overboard and bailing water out of the hold so the ship would not sink.

In times of crisis, pirates had to take such actions quickly. This was also true during battle. Therefore, although pirates spent many days at sea coping with boredom, filth, illness, and other problems, they still had to remain in good enough mental and physical shape to respond immediately in a crisis.

Chapter Three

Pillage and Plunder

M ost pirates did not mind dealing with the difficulties of long sea voyages as long as they were reward-
ed for their efforts. Their goal was to find vessels that
might be carrying gold and silver pieces, paper money,
jewelry, gemstones, rare spices, and other valuables. In the
process, they also robbed merchant ships of linens,
clothes, food, medical supplies, and ship gear like ropes
and anchors.

Finding the Right Victims

It was not always easy, however, to find ships to rob.
Sometimes pirates spent weeks at sea without seeing a
promising target. Other times they wasted time,
ammunition, and manpower attacking vessels that had
no treasures. For example, Calico Jack Rackam and his
pirate crew spent two years attacking ships in the West
Indies but came away with little of value. From one
ship they took only "50 Rolls of Tobacco, and Nine
Bags of Piemento [a kind of red pepper]." [6]

On many pirate ships the crew voted on where to
look for treasure. One popular place was the Indian

Ocean, where merchant vessels from England and Europe routinely carried gold and silver to buy spices, silk, slaves, and other goods from Africa and the Orient. Even more popular was the Spanish Main, the waters near the northern coast of South America. In this area, Spanish treasure

Pirates set out to rob a Spanish ship (background) by attacking it.

ships routinely carried silver coins and bars from South American mines to Spain. Pirates captured one such ship carrying 350,000 pieces of eight.

The most successful pirate captains working in the Spanish Main and elsewhere commanded several vessels rather than just one. For example, Bartholomew Roberts, who captured over four hundred ships in four years, had four ships with 508 crewmen under his command. One ship had forty-two guns and the others sixteen to thirty guns each. Blackbeard usually had a fleet of three ships carrying 415 men and fifty-two guns. Roberts and Blackbeard did not combine their forces, but other pirates did join their fleets to increase their chances of success.

Torture

Whether a lone merchant ship came upon a pirate fleet or just a single ship flying a pirate flag, it almost always surrendered without firing a shot. The reason for this was fear. Pirates had a

A captive, forced to walk the plank, is sent to his death.

reputation for torturing the captains of ships that did not surrender quickly. For instance, one witness said of a captured captain, "They put a Rope around his Neck and hoisted him up and down . . . til he was almost dead."[7]

In fact, some pirate crews tortured and killed any captains they caught, remembering the cruel captains they had once served on merchant or naval ships. Others asked the crew of the captured ship whether their captain deserved to live and spared his life only on that crew's request. Pirates might also torture and/or kill other people on board the captured ship, including passengers.

Weapons

Once pirates came on board a captured vessel, they were hard to resist because they were well armed. Almost all pirates carried pistols. In fact, because these handguns needed to be reloaded after firing only one shot, many pirates carried several. Blackbeard always had six pistols in holsters slung across his chest.

Many pirates carried a musket as well. Some pirates were so skilled at shooting this rifle that they could hit a man on another ship even when their own ship was rocking violently. Pirates also carried **cutlasses** (curved swords) and daggers (short knives) to kill men at close range.

Pirates used cannons to fire at ships from a distance, although they had to be careful not to sink their targets in the process. Each cannon could be loaded with one or two metal balls. Two balls linked by a chain were called chain shot, which was fired at a ship to

Using muskets, knives, pistols, and cutlasses pirates easily overcame their targets.

destroy its mast. To hurt the crew rather than the ship, pirates fired grapeshot, which consisted of tin cans filled with tiny metal balls, nails, and pieces of metal.

The Attack

Before starting an attack, pirates usually followed their victims for several days, looking through spyglasses to decide what kind of treasure and weapons might be on board. Some merchant ships were heavily armed, but others had false gunholes in their sides to appear as though they had more cannons than they really did. Therefore, pirates never knew what kind of resistance to expect.

However, pirates were not afraid of a fight. Once they decided to attack a ship, they rarely gave up. One of the worst sea battles between a pirate ship and its victim lasted over four hours. The pirate ship, the *Trompeuse*, had thirty guns and 250 pirates; its opponent, the *Bauden*, had sixteen guns and 68 men. During the battle, the two ships exchanged gunfire at extremely short range. Then the pirates roped the two ships together and tried to board the *Bauden*, but more gunfire kept them at bay. Finally the pirate ship was so shot full of holes that it began leaking heavily, so the pirates gave up and sailed away. Over 60 of the pirates had been killed during the battle, but only eight men

Pirates had no fear of attacking other ships and rarely gave up a fight.

(including the captain) were killed on the *Bauden*. In most cases, however, pirate ships won such attacks, boarding their opponents' vessel quickly and forcing a surrender.

Dividing the Spoils

Once pirates captured a ship, they divided its cargo according to the rules of their ship. On many vessels the loot was divided into equal shares, with each crewman getting one share, the captain two to six shares, and quartermaster two shares. First, however, the most valuable members of the crew were paid bonuses. For example, the carpenter might be given one hundred pieces of eight and the ship's surgeon two hundred pieces of eight.

Pirates who had been injured in battle also got additional money, in an amount depending on their wounds. On several ships, the loss of a right arm was

A pirate's rank determined how much treasure he received.

worth six hundred pieces of eight; a left arm or right leg, five hundred pieces of eight; a left leg, four hundred pieces of eight; and an eye or finger, one hundred pieces of eight. Such injuries were common, so it was not unusual to see a line of pirates with wooden legs and eye patches accepting their injury pay.

Bold Actions

In some places, pirates sailed away from a vessel before dividing up their loot because they feared getting caught if they remained nearby. In the Caribbean, however, they had no such fears; in the early 1700s only four naval warships and two naval sloops policed the area. The governor of Jamaica complained about this shortage, saying, "There is hardly one ship or vessel, coming in or going out of this island that is not plundered [by pirates]."[8]

Many other areas also had shortages of naval vessels because after a war between England, France, and Spain ended in 1713 these countries reduced their military forces. In England, for example, the Royal Navy was reduced from 53,785 ships in 1703 to 13,430 ships in 1715—not enough to police all of the waters where pirates sailed. Moreover, the reduction in naval ships put thousands of sailors out of work, and many of these unemployed seamen turned to piracy. The same thing had occurred after fifty years of fighting between England and Spain came to an end in 1603.

Although men turned to piracy to become rich, most pirates spent their fortunes as fast as they made

England's Royal Navy did not have enough ships to police all the waters that pirates sailed.

them. After weeks at sea they sailed into ports that welcomed pirates, then wasted their money on alcohol, gambling, and other forms of entertainment. Sometimes they committed robberies in these ports as well, trying to recoup some of the money they had lost. To some pirates, it seemed like they would never amass enough money to feel successful.

Chapter Four

Pirates on Shore

Pirates went ashore often to sell stolen goods and buy supplies. Sometimes they had to sneak into a town to get what they wanted, afraid of being arrested for piracy. Most of the time, however, they visited towns that openly welcomed pirates.

Profiting from Piracy

Towns that decided to welcome pirates did so because it was profitable. For instance, the pirate town of Port Royal on the Caribbean island of Jamaica became extremely wealthy by hosting pirates. Out of its nearly eight thousand residents, most earned a living by serving pirates. There were over forty-four tavern keepers selling drinks and food to pirates in Port Royal and numerous craftsmen who worked to convert stolen merchant ships into pirate ships. In addition, the town had many merchants eager to buy the pirates' loot, which included slaves stolen from slave-trading ships traveling from Africa to the New World.

Towns that harbored pirates benefited in another way as well: They were rarely attacked. For example,

Taverns were just one of many businesses that became wealthy by hosting pirates.

Spain and France wanted to take over Jamaica, which was the property of England, but, with hundreds of pirate ships usually anchored in the Port Royal harbor, their forces never dared attack. Meanwhile, many pirates used Port Royal as a starting point for attacks on Spanish treasure ships and settlements, which delighted the English. From 1655 to 1661, Port Royal pirates also attacked Spanish colonists in the central part of the island, looting eighteen cities, four towns, and thirty-six settlements.

Madagascar

Meanwhile, pirates operating in the Indian Ocean typically used the island of Madagascar as a base. Twice the size of Great Britain, Madagascar had many good harbors and at least two large pirate colonies. Among seamen of the eighteenth century, rumors abounded about how grand these colonies were.

In fact, most people believed that Madagascar's pirates had created a kingdom called Libertalia on the island, where they made their own rules and lived like kings. One rumor was that the wives of Libertalia's

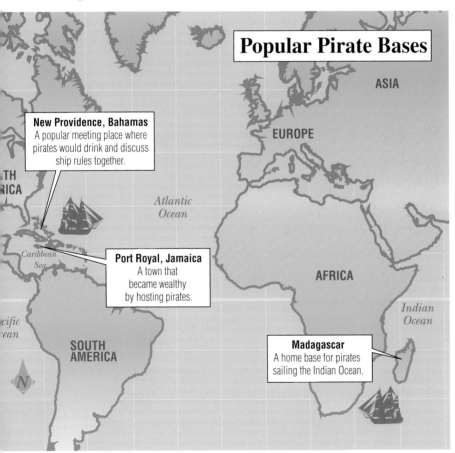

Popular Pirate Bases

ASIA

EUROPE

New Providence, Bahamas
A popular meeting place where pirates would drink and discuss ship rules together.

TH
RICA

Atlantic Ocean

Caribbean Sea

Port Royal, Jamaica
A town that became wealthy by hosting pirates.

AFRICA

Indian Ocean

cific ean

SOUTH AMERICA

Madagascar
A home base for pirates sailing the Indian Ocean.

N

pirates "were dressed in richest silks and some of them had diamond necklaces."[9]

However, reports from those who had visited Madagascar said that Libertalia did not exist and that most of the island's pirates were "very poor and despicable, even to the natives, among whom they had married."[10] Some said that only sixty to seventy pirates lived on the island, rather than the hundreds of pirates said to live there.

New Providence

A much larger pirate base was on the island of New Providence in the Bahamas. Pirate captains operating along the coast of North America and in the Caribbean used this island as a meeting place during the eighteenth century, which is one reason why many pirate ships at that time had similar rules. The pirates of New Providence discussed their ships' policies while drinking together.

New Providence had dozens of taverns along the beach of its main harbor, which could hold five hundred pirate ships. Beside the harbor was the town of Nassau, known for its strong alcoholic beverages. One of the pirates' favorites was bombo, or bumboo, a mixture of rum, water, sugar, and nutmeg. Another favorite drink was Rumfustian, a mixture of raw eggs, sugar, sherry, gin, and beer. A favorite New Providence food was "Solomon Grundy," or salamagundi, a salad made of cabbage, pickled onions, grapes, olives, hard-boiled eggs, and pieces of fish, turtle, shellfish, and any available meat, all mixed with a marinade of spiced wine, oil, garlic, herbs, and palm hearts.

Like all pirate havens, Nassau was also a rough place, where robberies and violence against both men and women were common. Honest men were few. Even the merchants of New Providence were thieves. They bought stolen goods from the pirates and then smuggled them into America, where it was illegal to conduct such trade.

Towns that welcomed pirates were rough places.

Getting Rid of Pirates

Eventually the governor of Virginia became frustrated that pirates were robbing honest merchants while dishonest merchants were profiting from the thefts. He complained to England that New Providence had become a "Nest of Pyrates"[11] that needed to be wiped out. Two years later England appointed a sea captain named Woodes Rogers as governor of the Bahamas and ordered him to do whatever was necessary to get rid of the pirates.

In July 1718, Rogers entered Nassau's harbor with a fleet of five heavily armed ships. The pirates quickly destroyed one of the ships, but Rogers was still able to take over the town. He offered pardons to over six hundred pirates who agreed to help him keep order in Nassau. Others were hunted down and executed. Rogers then stationed soldiers in the town to keep pirates from reclaiming the harbor.

Eventually other pirate towns suffered the same fate as Nassau. One by one, various government forces moved in to clear out the pirates. For example, England's Royal Navy established a base in Port Royal, and the town became known for its pirate executions. Calico Jack Rackam was hanged there, as were many other notorious pirates between 1720 and 1825.

Famous Deaths

As the forces against the pirates grew stronger, some of the most famous pirate captains died in battle. Bartholomew Roberts, for instance, was mortally wounded during a sea battle off the west coast of Africa. His men then threw him overboard at his request, so he would not be taken prisoner. Blackbeard also died in a battle, after

Bartholomew Roberts was killed after his ship (top left) was attacked. Blackbeard (bottom) also died in battle.

the governor of Virginia sent two heavily armed ships to catch him in 1717. Once Blackbeard was killed, his head was cut off and was mounted on one of the warships as a warning to other pirates.

Such warnings were not unusual. After one of the most famous pirates, Captain William Kidd, was hanged in England in 1701, his body was hung in chains beside the Thames River to show others that piracy would be harshly punished.

However, Kidd's death only made people more interested in piracy. The reason for this was buried treasure. Many rumors held that before Kidd was captured he hid some of his riches on an island off New York. After his execution, many men began searching for buried treasure there. None was ever found, but the idea that pirates buried their treasure began appearing in many novels, such as *Treasure Island* by Robert Louis Stevenson.

Heroic Figures

Such novels portrayed pirates as attractive or even heroic figures, downplaying or ignoring the harm they caused others. This led people to forget that most pirates were cruel thieves who tortured their victims and wasted their money on alcohol, gambling, and other pleasures. As author Frank R. Stockton wrote in the late nineteenth century,

> When I was a boy I strongly desired to be a pirate, and the reason for this was the absolute independence of that sort of life. Restrictions of all sorts had

Many popular stories have portrayed pirates as heroic rather than fearsome.

become onerous to me, and in my reading of the adventures of the bold sea-rovers of the [Spanish] main, I had unconsciously selected those portions of a pirate's life which were attractive to me, and had totally disregarded all the rest.[12]

By the time the pirate became a heroic figure rather than a fearsome one, the golden age of piracy had come to an end. Still, pirates continued to exist, although in far fewer numbers. Even today, small bands of modern pirates rob yachts and other small boats in remote seas, usually killing the vessels' passengers in the process. So long as there is money to be made from piracy, there will be ruthless people who take up the profession.

Notes

Chapter One: The Ship and Its Crew

1. Quoted in David Cordingly, *Under the Black Flag: The Romance and the Reality of Life Among the Pirates*. New York: Random House, 1995, p. 13.
2. Quoted in David Botting, *The Seafarers: The Pirates*. Arlington, VA: Time-Life Books, 1978, p. 47.
3. Quoted in Botting, *The Seafarers*, p. 161.

Chapter Two: The Rigors of Life at Sea

4. Quoted in Cordingly, *Under the Black Flag*, p. 99.
5. John Esquemeling, *The Buccaneers of America*. Glorieta, NM: Rio Grande, 1992, pp. 394–95.

Chapter Three: Pillage and Plunder

6. Quoted in Botting, *The Seafarers*, p. 26.
7. Quoted in Botting, *The Seafarers*, p. 60.
8. Quoted in Cordingly, *Under the Black Flag*, p. 107.

Chapter 4: Pirates on Shore

9. Cordingly, *Under the Black Flag*, p. 147.
10. Cordingly, *Under the Black Flag*, p. 147.
11. Quoted in David Cordingly, ed., *Pirates: Terror on the High Seas—from the Caribbean to the South China Sea*. Atlanta, GA: Turner, 1996, p. 108.
12. Frank R. Stockton, *Buccaneers and Pirates of Our Coast*. New York: Macmillan, 1928, p. 1.

Glossary

bosun: Also known as a boatswain, the person responsible for the maintenance and use of all ropes and rigging.

cutlass: A curved sword.

flogging: Whipping.

gunner: The person responsible for maintaining a ship's weapons and managing its ammunition.

hardtack: A dry, hard biscuit.

piece of eight: A Spanish silver coin, or peso, stamped with the number 8, because it was worth eight of a monetary unit called a real.

privateer: A pirate hired by one country to attack the sailing vessels of another.

quartermaster: A pirate captain's assistant, responsible for getting supplies, dividing them up, and also for administering punishments.

scurvy: A common shipboard illness caused by a lack of vitamin C.

ship: A sailing vessel with square sails and three or more masts.

sloop: A one-masted sailing vessel.

For Further Exploration

Robert E. Lee, *Blackbeard the Pirate: A Reappraisal of His Life and Times.* Winston-Salem, NC: John F. Blair, 1974.

Marine Research Society, *The Pirates Own Book: Authentic Narratives of the Most Celebrated Sea Robbers.* New York: Dover 1993.

Jennifer Marx, *Pirates and Privateers of the Caribbean.* Malabar, FL: Kriegor, 1992.

Karen McWilliams, *Pirates.* New York: Franklin Watts, 1989.

Richard Platt, *Eyewitness Books: Pirate.* New York: Alfred A. Knopf, 1994.

David Reinhardt, *Pirates and Piracy.* New York: Konecky & Konecky, 1997.

Robert C. Ritchie, *Captain Kidd and the War Against the Pirates.* Cambridge, MA: Harvard University Press, 1986.

Jan Rogozinski, *Pirates! An A–Z Encyclopedia.* New York: Da Capo, 1996.

Robert Louis Stevenson, *Treasure Island.* New York: Charles Scribner's Sons, 1981.

Rachel Wright, *Pirates.* New York: Franklin Watts, 1991.

Jane Yolen, *Pirates in Petticoats.* Philadelphia, PA: David McKay, 1963.

Index

About the Author

Patricia D. Netzley received a bachelor's degree in English from the University of California at Los Angeles (UCLA). After graduation she worked as an editor at the UCLA Medical Center, where she produced hundreds of medical articles, speeches, and pamphlets. She has written several dozen books for children and adults. Her books for Lucent's Mystery Library series include *UFOs*, *The Curse of King Tut, Witches,* and *Haunted Houses.* Her hobbies are weaving, knitting, and needlework. She and her husband, Raymond, live in southern California with their children, Matthew, Sarah, and Jacob.